Joaquín Yarza Luaces

Bosch
and Flemish Painting (15th century)

Fundación Amigos del Museo del Prado

Floor plan of the Prado Museum

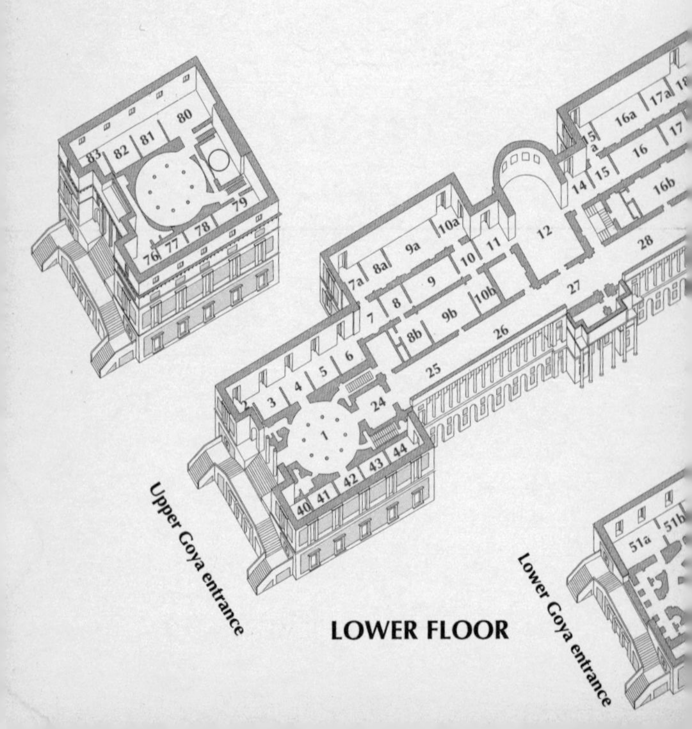

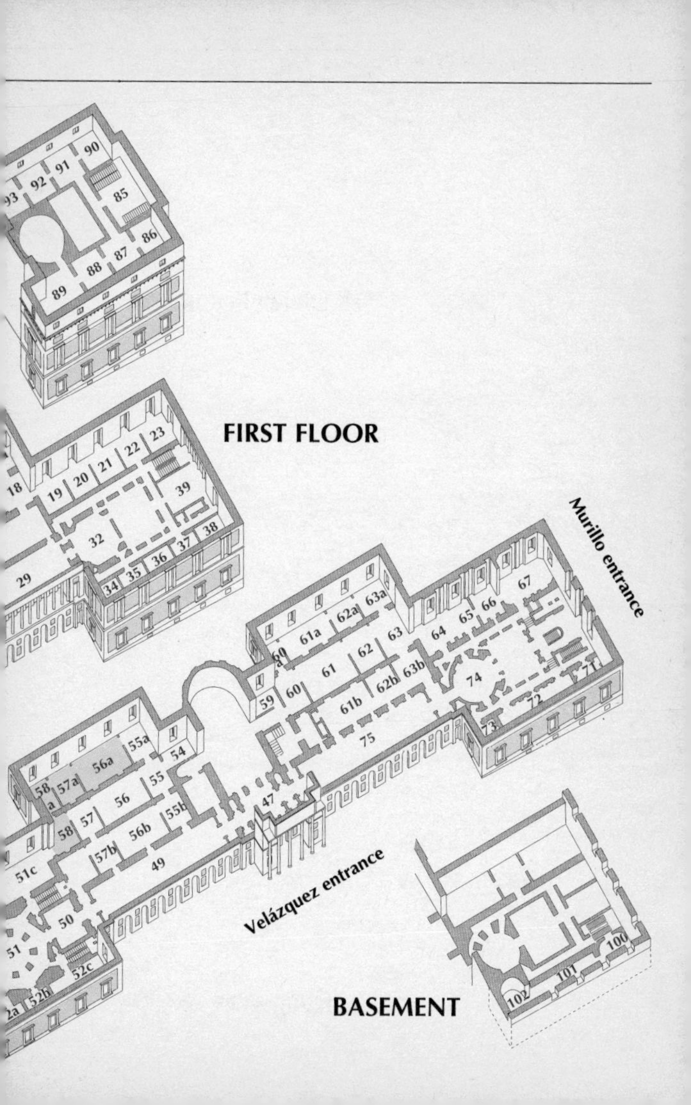

FIRST FLOOR
BASEMENT
Murillo entrance
Velázquez entrance
90
91
92
85
86
87
88
89
23
22
21
20
19
18
39
38
37
36
35
34
32
29
67
66
65
64
63a
62a
61a
60a
63
62
61
60
59
63b
62b
61b
74
71
72
73
75
55a
54
56a
57a
58a
55
56
57
58
55b
56b
57b
47
49
51c
50
51
52c
52b
52a
100
101
102

Third edition: 2002

Cover and interior design by Ángel Uriarte
Translation by John Pownall
Axonometric projections by Ana Pazó Espinosa
Edition by Carmen Ponce de León and Manuel Florentín
Layout by Antonio Martín

ISBN: 84-95452-03-0
Depósito legal: M-8.359-2002
Printed in Closas-Orcoyen, S.L. Paracuellos de Jarama (Madrid)
Printed in Spain

Introduction

It is a pity that Fifteenth-century Low Countries painting is often called 'Flemish primitive', because calling it 'primitive' makes us think of something at its outset which, in turn, gives rise to the notion of first steps being taken and this, alas, suggests that this something might still be rather raw, awkward, naive, or lacking in polish. Which is exactly and for long enough what many savants intended 'primitive' to mean when the Flemish School was spoken about, for it was being compared with Renaissance ideals of Art by people still hidebound in the belief that all things medieval had to be gothickly gloomy and ignorant in everything. For such luminaries, this school's period had been no more than an interlude of charming artists who painted on wood and, fine craftsmen that they were, had even managed to invent oil painting, but, when considered as a school, had fallen so very far short of that perfection, that sense of perspective, that rightness which was the hall mark of the Italian Renaissance. Which is, of course, nothing but nonsense. By the time this splendid school came into its own, the Low Countries had already long enjoyed an artistic tradition that could boast Romanesque illuminated books and 'international' Gothic amongst its own and the World's major achievements.

To add insult to injury, even to-day we persist in our use of the term 'Flemish' even though Flanders is but that part of the Low Countries where the important cities of Bruges and Ghent stand. Brabant is in no wise Flanders, yet Antwerp and Brussels, even s'Hertogenbosch, the town where Hieronymus Bosch was born and grew up in, form part of it. Robert Campin and Weyden were both from Hainault. A part is plainly being taken for the whole, and this 'whole' should be properly called the Low Countries or Netherlands. But in Spain and many places else, the term 'Flemish' has been used since the 16th century which would make changing it a bind though it would be as well to bear in mind that, when using it, we are displaying an ignorance which, for once, is not 'gothick'.

The Low Countries in the 15th Century combined a series of factors that played their part in giving rise to an important school of painting there. The country, originally a patchwork of minor states, gradually fell under the sway of the

Duke of Burgundy. One of Europe's most densely-populated areas at the time, it also had a higher-than-average number of city dwellers. Bruges, Ghent, Amsterdam, Tournai, and Brussels were wealthy urban centres blessed with merchants of repute and outstanding craftsmen in many different trades. When Philip the Good inherited the duchy after his father John the Fearless's violent death, he had the capital moved from Dijon in Burgundy up to the Low Countries. Prior to this and from about 1380 onwards, it now seems clear that a host of artists (painters, miniaturists, sculptors) had not only worked in the Low Countries themselves, but had been busily spreading their influence out to the great northern European centres of Paris and Dijon. With the fall of Paris to the English in the Hundred Years' War however ,it ceased to be the great artistic capital it had once been, and a similar fate befell Dijon once the Duke moved his residence up to the northern cities. As a result, those who had once been tempted south stayed put and worked for them and their court, the urban middle class, or for the great european dealers (in the main Spanish or Italian) who were coming to value their style more and more.

At this time Robert Campin was living in Tournai as was Hubert van Eyck in Ghent. Jan van Eyck, Hubert's younger brother, was soon to make his appearance on the scene. It was they more than anyone else who revolutionized the painting of their times by perfecting the use of oils, an advance that had profound and lasting consequences for the finished work by making possible the use of colour tones of such purity and intensity that astonishing light effects, hitherto impossible, became part of their stock in trade. These giant strides in both technique and the uses to which it was put found no equal in the self-absorbed and intellectual nature of what was going on at the same time in Tuscany. Up north, there was no yearning for the models of Antiquity , anymore than there was any questioning of the notion that an artist was, first and foremost, a mastercraftsman whose output was still to be approached as it had been in its late medieval sense. True, Jan van Eyck had a lively sense of his own importance as a mastercraftsman and did sign almost all of his paintings while the rest of his European counterparts, including the Tuscans, as yet did not. His art was indeed very conceptual and crammed with symbols at times disguised by a veneer of everyday simplicity but never privately so. His main clients were Philip the Good and those around him although he did work for many others, including Italian merchants who kept a house in Bruges, the place he himself lived in longest. He is one of the greatest portrait painters ever, be it for the honesty of his realism, his clear-eyed vision of his sitters or the symbolic framework within which he sets them.Though his paintings now hang in great museums throughout the world, the Prado has but one that can be attributed to him: *The Fountain of Grace.*

Another artist who seems to have been a contemporary of the van Eycks and in close contact with Roger van der Weyden was long known as the Master of Flemalle. With time, he was gradually identified as Robert Campin, a painter from Tournai and van Weyden's master. Though older than Jan van Eyck, he outlived him by several years. There is no general agreement about his identity even now-a-days and his work is still anonymously attributed, mainly because his paintings tie in more with Brussels than Tournai. He chose to paint for the Tournai middle class rather than its great families. Not only was he active here as a painter but also as a public figure and the latter brought with it more than one headache for him. The Prado has four of his works, three of which are undoubtably his and cover the artist's earliest efforts on through to his more mature later paintings which share certain qualities to be found in the work of younger artists such as Eyck and Weyden.

In the next generation, Petrus Christus is to be found living in Brussels and following in van Eyck's footsteps. The Prado has a charming *Virgin and Child by him.* Tournai lost artistic standing when its best painter, Roger van Weyden, moved on to Brussels, although Robert Campin, his most faithful disciple, still painted his style. There are few catalogued works from this artist and The Prado has none of these. As time went by, this city was quickly to become an important art centre even though Bruges was still the focus of international trade. Weyden was made Official Painter to the city which added much to the prestige of that post. While van Eyck was known for making art symbolic, complex, and intellectual, van Weyden lent it his immediacy, expressivity and feelings. Many of his compositions became models of reference throughout the Low Countries as they later were to do throughout Europe. He was very highly esteemed in Spain where, by the 1440's, the king, Juan III of Castile, already owned one of his major works: the *Miraflores Triptych.* The Prado can boast what many consider to be his masterpiece and one of the greatest works of European art: *The Descent from the Cross.* After his death, his official post went to an obscure artist called Vrancke van der Stockt, some of whose paintings were long mistaken for van de Weydens, which speaks well for their quality. This is even more noteworthy if it is born in mind that his rival was none other than Pieter, the son of Rodger, van der Weyden and heir to his studio, a considerable painter in his own right if the attributing to him of some hitherto anonymous work is correct.

Bouts, coming down from the north, set up in Louvain, where he was honoured with a post like that given Weyden in Brussels. This city, though less populous than the others, was a centre of learning and commerce. The *Triptych of the Last Supper* at St. Peter's Cathedral in Louvain and the paintings for the town hall are amongst his finest

works, while the Prado's early *Polyptych of Christ's Childhood is yet another.*
Ghent was perhaps the most highly populated city of the era and an important artistic centre in its own right. Unfortunately the Prado has nothing by the artists who worked there, artists of the stamp of the hitherto little-known and only recently rediscovered Justus of Ghent and the admirable and disquieting Hugo van der Goes.
The last thirty years of the century saw the flourishing of still more artistic centres and the host of artists who worked in them. Few further advances were made on the work of the founding masters (van Eyck, Campin, Weyden), who were still held up as models to revere and even imitate. At best, a few changes in the concept of landscape are worthy of note but even these are not because any more profound effects honed on the feelings, as in van Eyck's work, but rather to different kinds of light becoming used to catch different times of the year or even hours of the day. Memling was by then the most popular artist of his age, choosing Bruges as his workplace and this despite its steadily growing signs of economic decline. His art is simple, warm, clean toned, not overdramatic and highly attractive but in no wise truly original. Among the Flemish masters of the XV Century he produced more than any other. He was commissioned more than once by the Hospital of St John which is now the main City Museum. He was German born.

It was not until the turn of the century that artists began to be fanned by the winds of change of the Italian Renaissance which, spreading now from Florence and out into Tuscany could by then truly be called Italian. A few from the North (such as Weyden) had already travelled to Italy but had not been over receptive to what they saw there whereas italian customers and even some painters had been awed by the great skill of these visitors' works. Much else had also undergone great changes. Upon Charles the Rash´s death, the duchy of Burgundy had been dissolved as such. the Low Countries suddenly found themselves but a part of a central european empire, due to marriage of the late duke's daughter to Emperor Maximillian I. The marriage of two of the sons of this match to two of Ferdinand and Isabella's children was soon to increase castilian influence in the Low Countries even further. Apart from the effect this was to have on Spanish painting, it had tremendous consequences for the northern countries.
During the reign of Emperor Charles V, lutheran reform found willing adepts among a few intellectual circles whose brand of humanism differed sharply from that of the Italians and is best typified by that of Erasmus of Rotterdam. Furthermore, urban development no longer followed the lines of that of the first half of the 14th Century. Antwerp and Brussels had become great cities with their own specific weight in all things, be these political or

artistic. This showed most in the fields of sculpture and tapestry-making, the centre of which had shifted first from Arras to Tournai, and then to Brussels to the virtual exclusion of everywhere else.

The Renaissance was accepted in fits and starts The great influence of the immediate past made change come about slowly. Artists started to realize the advantages to making a journey to Italy, either at their own expense or as part of the entourage of some important person. Others, less fortunate, learnt of what was happening there through Italian painters (such as Solario and Vincidor) who came north to settle or spend some time in the cities, or through such paintings, tapestries and drawings as were brought back from the Italy by those who had travelled. Nevertheless, some artists whose Italian sketchbooks and notebooks showed their openness to new ideas, still remained faithful in their works to their own rich Flemish tradition and this should never be understood as a failing on their part, given thats their own native tradition was still very much alive and on-going. Even those artists who spearheaded change never fully gave up on their native craftsmanship nor that taste for fine detail and realism that so often distinguished both their portraits and landscapes.

Gerard David, who was still at Bruges in the first two decades of the 16th century, was still essentially a 15th-century artist. He was a vastly successful and had an ample catalogue of paintings to his name. The Prado owns one unquestionable original *(The Rest on the Flight to Egypt)* and two *Virgins of more doubtful attribution.* Hieronymus Bosch was indeed a man apart, but even his vision of the world was beyond question medieval and his technique stayed true to its glorious Flemish traditions. He enjoyed fame in the Low Countries while still alive and could count among his admirers patrons of the standing of Phillip the Fair and Margaret of Austria Nassau. His name even reached far of Venice where some very singular works of his are still to be found. Thanks to the high esteem the Guevaras held him in but more to that of Philip II, the Prado can boast the best collection in the world of this painter's relatively limited output of masterworks, outstanding among these being his two large-scale triptychs, his *Garden of Earthly Delights* and *Epiphany,* though his *Seven Deadly Sins* and *Hay-Wain* are also wonders in themselves.

Room 58 (LVIII)

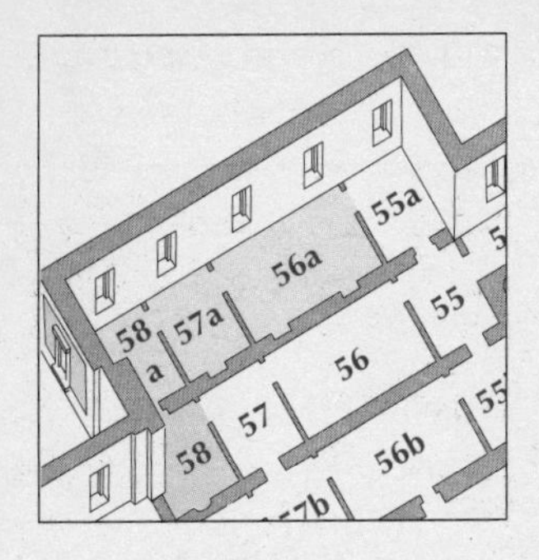

PETRUS CHRISTUS
Virgin and Child

DIERICK OR THIERRY BOUTS. POLYPTYCH
Annunciation, Visitation, Nativity, Adoration of the Magi

ALBERT BOUTS (?)
Head of Christ

ROGER VAN DER WEYDEN
The Descent from the Cross

ROBERT CAMPIN
Annunciation

ROBERT CAMPIN
St. John the Baptist and Heinrich von Werl

St. Barbara

ROBERT CAMPIN
Betrothal of the Virgin

PETRUS CHRISTUS
Virgin and Child
(Cat. No. 1921)

Christus is a little-known artist overshadowed by Jan van Eyck his predecessor and perhaps, though indirectly, his teacher. Nevertheless, his scant output has of late undergone a reappraisal. Although Christus's work took after van Eyck's in many ways, it does display its own interesting persona and much excellent craftsmanship. Christus arrived in Bruges shortly after van Eyck's death, there to become a noteworthy painter until his own death. The small panel in the Prado comes from a convent in Piedrahíta (Ávila, Spain) probably done during the middle years of his career (c. 1460-1465). It portrays the Virgin on a throne, about to be crowned 'Regina Cœli' ('Queen of Heaven') by an angel. The Child's nakedness symbolizes his humanity, though he holds the globe of the world in his hand. Some claim it to be based on a now-lost original by Weyden. The background landscape is very beautiful, but the artist has committed an inexplicable mistake in the perspective: the wall behind the right-hand part of the arch is part of a house that then ceases to exist in the next arch along to the right.

DIERICK OR THIERRY BOUTS. POLYPTYCH:
Annunciation, Visitation, Nativity, Adoration of the Magi
(Cat. No. 1461)

It seems that Bouts came from Haarlem, then in the north of the Low Countries and now Holland, but set himself up in Louvain, where he eventually earned himself the post of official town painter in his later years (1468-1475) though 17th Century records do show him keeping on a house in Haarlem for many years as well. This has led to the belief that he also ran a studio there at some time. The Prado Museum's polyptych may have come down to us from those early years of his career. Although Bouts´personal style made figures tall, solemn, stiff, and somewhat inexpressively whispy, he admired the art of van Eyck and young van der Weyden.

In this set of four paintings, each scene is set off by an

architectural facade painted with a grisaille archway or archivolt with figures taken from Weyden as in that master's *Miraflores Triptych* (Berlin Mus.). There are, however, several variations that make it more a re-interpreting than a mere copy. The sequence has to do with Mary and the birth of Jesus and highlights her role in the Redemption. This contrasts with the pictures on the archivolts that begin with the creation of Adam and Eve, Sin, and God's wrath above the panel of the Annunciation, thus keeping alive the time hallowed medieval custom of counter-positioning Eve with Mary. The other archivolts offer a broad panorama of the Pas-

sion and Resurrection. The broad landscape, far from the every-day bustle of urban life, is what stands out most in the Visitation In the middle ground and to the right there is a Flemish inn of the period. The annunciation has in its sham archivaults the cycles of the Creation and Fall whereas the Annunciation and Nativity's show a thorough-going Passion cycle running from the betrayal by Judas and on to the Resurrection. The Epiphany is framed within a vision of Christ Triumphant amongst the symbols of his Power. Recent cleaning has brought to light both the work's skilful workmanship and the qualities of its colours and glazing.

ALBERT BOUTS (?) **Head of Christ** (Cat. No. 2698)

Dierick Bouts had two sons who became painters. The second was Albert, who is identified with the outstanding Master of the Assumption of the Virgin of Brussels. He came of age about 1480. It would seem that he died in 1549, unless he has been confused with another painter of the same name, which could well be as he otherwise would have lived to an amazingly ripe old age. The imagery of the picture follows his father's though it came to be more highly regarded if we go by the number of copies and imitations of it still in existence. This is due to its being an especially expressive icon that was ideal for both churches and private places of worship.

ROGER VAN DER WEYDEN
The Descent from the Cross (Cat. No. 2825)

Though a masterpiece in the history of painting, this is no more than the middle section of a three-piece triptych, the laterals to which have been lost. It was commissioned for the chapel of the Brotherhood of Crossbowmen in the church of Notre-Dame Extramuros in Louvain. In the 1500's it was acquired by Queen Mary of Hungary, and then found its way into Philip II of Spain's collection in the monastery of El Escorial, where it was to remain from 1547 until 1939. It is most probably an early work of the painter's newly-found maturity (1432-1435) for his master, Robert Campin's influence is still evident, so strongly so, that some scholars have claimed that is was painted by Campin himself. We can be certain however that it reached El Escorial with both laterals attached and that one was of the four Evangelists, and the other of the Resurrection. Both have disappeared. Which is odd in itself and could mean that the facts here might have become a bit mixed up, for thoughe a triptych of these characteristics could easily depict the Resurrection on one side, it makes little sensee that it would portray the four Evangelists on the other when what was traditionally called for was a scene such as Christ on the road to Calvary. This could well be a latter, though period, addition.

No other work gives a stronger feel of sculpture painted. The golden background tone is darkened by shadows that seem thrown by the figures, thus reinforcing their sculptural feel and the optical illusion. This impression is strengthened by the presence of tracery imitating gilt wood at the corners. The tremendous bodyliness of each figure and the sharp shading confirm the idea that Weyden consciously conceived of his painting in this way, as he was to do in some few more as well. The nearly life-like scale in no way

diminishes from that exacting precision in which the very the tears glisten as intensely as facts. Both for their expressiveness and execution, the hands of Christ and the Virgin are amongst the most moving details to be found in Flemish art. Enclosing the composition within a sort of ellipse argues a painstaking eye for small details and this, in turn, to the end of establishing an immediate bridge between form and content. This is whys the lifeless and inert body of Christ sprawls in similar wise to that of his collapsed Mother, the fact that one of their arms and hands look so alike proclaiming their double Passion, that of the Son and that of the Mother. Both figures are stamped with a such a marked personality that they eventually became prototypes that were copied again and again in later works. In the same wise, the richly attired figure that holds Christ's feet and is taken to be Joseph of Arimethea has such a clearly defined and characterful face that this has been said to portray a man who, though dead when Weyden did the work, had been known to him. Besides the major figures there are other secondary ones such as the boy on the ladder in the central section who can be identified, though that of the man behind Joseph of Arimethea and carrying a pot of balm cannot. The skull and cross bones motif on the little rug on the floor bears witness to the belief that the Crucifixion took place on the Hill of the Skull which in turn harks back to the earlier belief that Adam had been buried there. This would then see the Crucifixion as fulfilling the promise made to Adam's son Seth at the Gates of Paradise. Furthermore, the emotional force of the painting is another source of Weyden's success. Being less cerebral than van Eyck, he was the better equipped to convey the spiritual to the average Christian at church as well as to those of greater intellectual discernment. Here, he makes much of this talent and yet does so with great sobriety.

ROBERT CAMPIN
Annunciation (Cat. No. 1915)

Very few of Robert Campin's works are still with us today, which makes the Prado's collection all the more stunning. This is perhaps the work that is attributed to him with the least certainty. Two other *Annunciations* exist: the *Mérode Trip-*

tych, New York, and Brussels Museum version. It was recently demonstrated that the *Mérode Triptych* is not wholly authentic and this despite having been accepted as such for long enough. The Prado's painting shows no trace of any underlying painting, which is grounds for suspicion to say the least, unless it can be shown to have been a copy or studio effort. There are however those who say it was done very early on in the master's career before van Eyck started painting or Weyden made his visit to his studio. There are, however, those who consider it to be by Daret, his disciple and painted while the master was still alive. Be that as it may, the work itself is of the first order with its iconographic complement of 'architectonic sculpture' figuring amongst these David as musician, Moses with the tablets of the Law that the Incarnation replaced or God as the Lord of the Universe.

ROBERT CAMPIN
St. John the Baptist and Heinrich von Werl
(Cat. No. 1513)
St. Barbara
(Cat. No. 1514)

These two may have been the wings of a triptych whose centre section has been lost. In the lower area of what would be the left-hand piece (the one of St. John) we find an inscription giving the date (1483) and the name of the person who commissioned the piece, Henry de Werl. This is one of Campin's most important pieces, the only dated one indicating who commissioned it. The resemblance of St. Barbara to Weyden's female characters has led some to say the master of Flemalle was not Robert Campin but the young van der Weyden. Now-a-days it is held to be an authentic

Campin though displaying the influence of the youngest and most creative of his disciples on a master who, though mature, was still open to fresh ideas. In the same way, the lay-out of the setting where Henry de Werl kneels and the presence of a mirror which reflects what is going on behind the viewer, are borrowings from van Eyck.

Heinrich von Werl was both a Provincial in the Minor Order of St. Francis and a well-known preacher. Records show him visiting Tournai, where Campin worked, during 1435 for certain. It is an exceptionally realistic and true-to-life portrait, one among the few the Prado has from that century and this despite the Flemish portrait's being in those times a tremendously important genre (Campin, van Eyck, Weyden, etc.). The grisaille Virgin against the background wall is in the 'International Gothic' style. The interior where St. Barbara is reading seems a typical comfortably middle-class home. It is the forebear of the realistic studies the painters of the Low Countries were later to so relish. Though full of signs of an apparently mundane life, these in themselves are supercharged with symbolism. If in the painting of Henry de Werl we find the Virgin, here, in the Saint Barbara, we have a Throne of Grace which represents the Trinity done in grisalle above the fireplace. The bunch of lilies, as in the Annunciation, signifies purity and alludes to the maidenhood of the Virgin. The saint's identity is made implicit by the background tower in which she had been incarcerated.

ROBERT CAMPIN
Betrothal of the Virgin
(Cat. No. 1887)

This is considered to be an early work done immediately after his *Seilern Triptych* (Courtauld Institute, London) and before he was influenced by other great masters. It is of higher craftsmanship than the *Assumption*. It is painted on both front and back, where vigorous grisaille pictures of Saint James the Greater and Saint Clare are to be found. The betrothal is set out in a very unusual way. On one side, the ceremony takes place in front of a Gothic

doorway under construction. This probably alludes to the New Testament and the imminence of Christ, this explaining why the arch is till unfinished. The archivaults of the gateway give pre-eminence to David possibly to thus underscore the true descent of Mary Virgin that more often begins with Jesse the great king's father, in other works. The characters portrayed are so vivid, so personality crammed as to seem, as in so many early Flemish works, true portraits whereas the Virgin in her depositions is altogether idealized and is a foretaste of how van der Weyden would soon or possibly already did express her. Utterly set aside from this and diagonally buried deep and over in the background, an exotic, finished temple can be seen in which the betrothal that will make Joseph into Mary's husband takes place. It is an ancient temple and brimming with Old Testament imagery such as that of its stained glass windows depicting the creation and the fall of Adam and Eve. This represents the Synagogue and the Old Testament. The other scenes, such as the Sacrifice of Isaac in sculptural, almost grisaille style, figure forth Christ's fate through techniques later and subtly to be used by van Eyck.

Room 58 a (LVIII a)

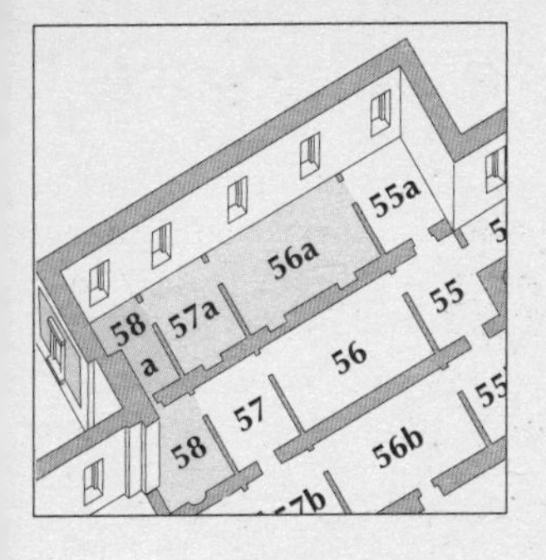

SCHOOL OF VAN EYCK
The Fountain of Grace

VRANCKE VAN DER STOCKT
Triptych of the Redemption

ROGER VAN DER WEYDEN
Pietà

ROGER VAN DER WEYDEN
Virgin and Child

ANONYMOUS BRUGES FOLLOWER OF VAN DER WEYDEN
Crucifixion

HANS MEMLING
Virgin and Child

HANS MEMLING
Triptych: **Nativity, Adoration of the Magi, Presentation of Christ in the Temple**

MASTER OF THE LEGEND OF ST. CATHERINE (?)
Crucifixion

SCHOOL OF VAN EYCK
The Fountain of Grace
(Cat. No. 1511)

At least two other copies exist of this unusual painting, both from the 16th century and both by Spanish artists. By 1455 it was already in Spain and had been donated to the monastery of El Parral in Segovia which was then under construction. It has been said to be an old copy of an original now lost and even seen to be an authentic van Eyck from his journeyman years. While it does have something of the *Polyptych of the Adoration of the Lamb* in Ghent in its spacious middle zone, it little resembles the master's manner of painting. The upper area with the Maiestas beneath the micro-architecture or canopy, flanked by the Virgin and John the Evangelist, is quite telling. At the foot of the throne is the sacrificial Lamb. From beneath it spring the waters that flow to the fountain which gives the painting its name. The eucharistic and yet apocalyptic nature of the painting is clear. On the banks of the waters, two communities take opposing stances. On the left (our left, since it is the right-hand side of the throne), the hosts of this Earth reverently approach the waters, attentive to the pope's gestures. On the right, the Sanhedrin, led by the high priest, spurns them with shocked gestures of outrage. This anti-Semitic element is not to be found in the Ghent altarpiece and yet is tellingly appropriate to the Castilians of the period in their bigoted war against jewish converts who were held to be forever, though secretly backsliders. The public debate held on various occasions turned upon the true identity of Jesus, the Jews refusing to see him as their Messiahs and rejecting salvation through the Eucharist. The robe of the High Priest, who here symbolizes the Synagogue, is rent in twain while the Rolls of the Law tumble to the floor. The blindfold he wears is that of he who will not see. To mark him out from the rest, he wears twelve gem stones on his chest and a mitre like that of a Christian Bishop, an article of headwear common to the dignitaries of most persuasions during the Lower Middle Ages in both France and Spain.

VRANCKE VAN DER STOCKT
Triptych of the Redemption
(Cat. Nos. 1888-89-90-91-92)

For many years this huge triptych was identified as part of the *Cambrai Altarpiece* commissioned from van der Weyden in 1454 and finished in 1459. But while a detailed stylistic analysis showed some similarities with the master of Tournai's style, many marked differences were patent as well. This led to Vrancke van der Stockt being considered its author, as he had succeeded Weyden as official painter in Brussels after his death in 1464. He and the Master of the Legend of St. Catherine, who was perhaps van der Weyden's son Peter, and the Master of the Embroidered Foliage were the master's most devoted disciples.

The centre of the open triptych represents a symbolic Crucifixion, like the one in Weyden's *Triptych of the Seven Sacraments* taking place at the entrance to a large church. The imagery should however be read from the left panel, with Adam and

Eve's fall in the background and their expulsion from paradise in the foreground. The Crucifixion hints at a redemption which can embrace a Judgement Day that overcomes Original Sin as is made explicit in the third panel. As to its overall composition, echoes of the Beaune *Judgement* by Weyden haunt the work. The centre piece also follows the lead of the previous master although they are more oval and less perfect in their execution. The chosen setting is the interior of a great gothic cathedral much like that used for Seven Sacraments triptych. The whole is framed by classical architectural forms within which an ample cycle of events are taking place that round out the dominant main panel's message. When closed, the triptych shows excellently painted figures in grisaille depicting the story of Jesus and the tribute money, with the Pharisees set up on stone pedestals that bear Gospel texts.

ROGER VAN DER WEYDEN
Pietà
(Cat. No. 2540)

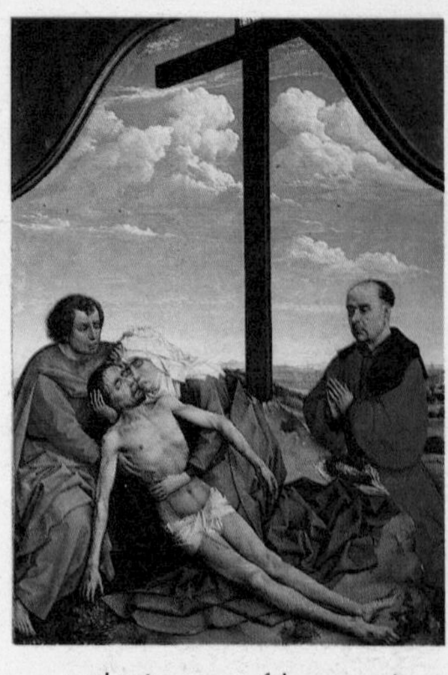

Authentic original, studio version, or plain copy? Four panels depicting this theme and layout are known to exist. The ones in London and Brussels are in landscape settings while the Prado's and the Berlin version have a portrait format. Doubts abound as to which is the original and this to such an extent that some believe all four are just copies of a lost Weyden prototype. The centre section showing the *pietà* derives from the same scene in the *Granada* and *Miraflores* triptychs. In some of these versions even the donor has been copied. The Prado's displays great craftsmanship though the underdrawing betrays its having been done from an original. It has also been probably cut down at the top as the format was for sure originally rectangular. The subject matter was tremendously popular during that century, and the donor's presence in the holy scene is a sign of his wish to make himself one with Jesus and Mary's sufferings.

ROGER VAN DER WEYDEN
Virgin and Child
(Cat. No. 2722)

Also known as the 'Durán Madonna' for its having belonged to Pedro Fernández-Durán until he left it to the Prado with the rest of his collection in 1931. Although it is undocumented, critics consider it to be an authentic and important work. It marks a break with Robert Campin's style and establishes another that was to be continued in later pieces, especially those by the so-called Master of the Embroidered Foliage, albeit almost none share the same plastic values as they are normally set out of doors. As hints towards his influence can be detected in the work of the Castile School of the second half of the XV Century, it would seem that he was also esteemed in Spain. Weyden was fond of highlighting his painted forms against dark backgrounds and framing them in tracery to point up his sculptural intent. The red of Mary's cloak is not just for aesthetic effect, even though the picture has also been called 'The Virgin in Red', for it is meant to intimate Jesus's future Passion. The angel about to crown the Virgin is a borrowing Jan van Eyck and is there to declare her as the Queen of Heaven. A few years back, the painting was vandalized but happily has been restored without any loss to its loveliness.

ANONYMOUS BRUGES FOLLOWER OF VAN DER WEYDEN
Crucifixion
(Cat. No. 1886)

A small panel of excellent quality based on an original by Weyden. In the 19th century it was credited as his, although earlier it had been attributed to Dürer because of its apocryphal signature and date of 1513. Today it is thought to be the work of someone who imitated the master's style during the early 16th century. The German artist's signature is not to be wondered at given his vast reputation. The painting shows very delicate colouring and considerable attention to detail. The stock images correspond to Weyden, especially the group of John and the Virgin, and Mary Magdalene, that have been copied, colour and line, from the museum's *Descent from the Cross*. It could be said that, as a whole, it is flawed by being patched up of parts that do not quite meld together within their new setting, each element having been lifted from a different source.

HANS MEMLING
Virgin and Child
(Cat. No. 2543)

Memling belonged to the last generation of 15th-century painters.In many ways, he was a forerunner of change as he softened the often severe stock character types of earlier generations. In doing so, he was able to please a wider audience, who were enchanted by the charm of his characterisations. He has however been belittled as lacking expressivity and skill enough to portray the grander emotions and dramatic situations that his times demanded. This little panel at the Prado, though rather ignored until quite recently, has been rehabilitated after its being displayed at the great exhibition in Bruges that marked the 500th anniversary of his death. It is one of many pictures of the Virgin and Child surrounded by angels playing music or entertaining Him. This type of Virgin is based on Weyden. The landscape in the background and the field in the foreground evoking the *locus amœnus* of medieval literature are richly rendered. Dated c. 1480, it is a work of the artist's full maturity. Though authentic, it has nevertheless suffered somewhat with time. It is a prime example of the world he set out to portray in order to satisfy those patrons who so readily accepted him.

HANS MEMLING. Triptych:
Nativity, Adoration of the Magi, Presentation of Christ in the Temple
(Cat. No. 1557)

This is one of Memling's masterpieces, now dated c. 1470. This would mean it was done nine years before the *Floreins Triptych* (St. John's Hospital, Bruges), which was commissioned by Floreins for a side altar in the hospital chapel and harked back to earlier works both in its composition and imagery. It is of great importance to the understanding of how the artist worked. The central piece was inspired by Weyden's *Columba Triptych*, especially in its the grouping of the Virgin, the Child, and the king kneeling at his feet. The Virgin and Child composition in the left-hand piece is very like the same grouping in the centre of Weyden's *Bladellin Triptych*, which makes it clear that Memling set but little store on originality as it does that Weyden was his favourite fount of inspiration. The spatial composition is quite interesting in being the same for the central and left-

hand pieces while the right-hand panel's has nothing to do with that of the others. Some hold that the group accompanying the Ethiopian king is taken from the same subject painted by Stefan Lochner in Cologne Cathedral. It should be remembered that Memling was indeed from Germany even though most of his work was done in Bruges. The fact that this was the first time in Flemish painting that the third king was represented as coloured is also worth noting. Though this had been occasionally done in Germanic painting, it was only since Memling's times that it has become a pictorial commonplace. The fact that almost all the triptych was reproduced on a smaller scale for Jan Floreins also bespeaks a uncommon degree of sheer craftsmanship in this artist's work. The panel itself may have reached Spain c. 1500. It once belonged to the Emperor Charles V and was kept in the castle of Aceca near Villaseca de la Sagra (Toledo, Spain).

MASTER OF THE LEGEND OF ST. CATHERINE (?)
Crucifixion (Cat. No. 2663)

The Museum still catalogues this panel as being by a disciple of Roger van der Weyden and is almost certainly right to do so. However and as E. Bermejo points out, it would seem more just to call this 'disciple' the Master of the Legend of St. Catherine. It is worth noting that many people believe the anonymous artist to have been Roger van der Weyden's son Pieter. Of him we know that he was born in 1437, was trained in his father's studio, that he set up on his own after his father's death, and then lived on until 1510. This interesting though second rank artist, whether Roger's son or not, has been credited with a number of excellent paintings that show the influence of Rodger quite clearly. Though some of his figures are more personalized in their features, they still hark back to Roger's stock of types. Here, part of the panel is a copy of the Crucifixion from the Mus. of Vienna's triptych, while the three women on the right are a more personal and thus ground breaking contribution by the Master of the Legend of St. Catherine.

Room 57 a (LVII a)

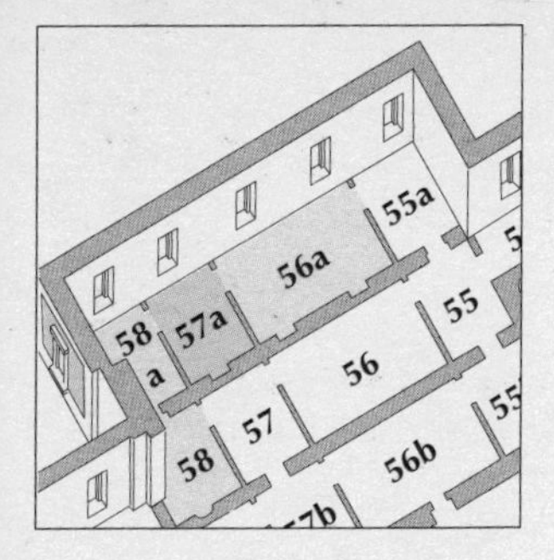

GERARD DAVID
Virgin and Child

GERARD DAVID
Rest on the Flight to Egypt

GERARD DAVID
Virgin and Child (Cat. No. 1537)

David was the last of the great Flemish late-Gothic painters, even though he had some inklings of the formal repertory of the Renaissance. Born in dutch Oudewater c. 1450-1460, he moved to Bruges, where he was acknowledged as a master in 1484. He lived there almost uninterruptedly until his death in 1523 and ran a large and successful studio there. He is credited with a great number of paintings full of a warm friendly manner that lacks the sharp edged precision of his predecessors thanks to his use of *sfumato* in his later work in the way that Isenbrandt had before him. He painted certain types of Virgin and Child figures so often that they became thorough-going popular icons. This painting is not in all certainty by his hand and was not listed in the last cataloguing of his work as one of them. It does reflect his manner to a certain degree however. It was kept at El Escorial until 1839.

GERARD DAVID
Rest on the Flight to Egypt
(Cat. No. 2643)

Apart from the Prado's, there are other works on this subject and its variations. Two of them may be studio versions (Metropolitan, New York) and a copy (Antwerp) of ours, while another lovely painting at the National Gal. in Washington only differs very slightly from it.He probably did it very late in his career, c. 1515. Very broadly based on the Apocrypha, or, more probably on tales stemming from these, it captures two moments of the Flight. First, as from the woods in the background, we see the Flight

itself, with Mary and the Child on an ass and Joseph following along behind on foot. The main scene however fills the foreground with its seated Virgin of the Milk, a charming figure based on models by Van Eyck. But it is the landscape which is really the subject of the work and which probably gives it its greatest pictorial impact. On the left a city can be seen, surely that which marked their journey's end in Egypt, a city that shows very little evidence of David's being receptive to Renaissance influences.

Room 56 a (LVI a)

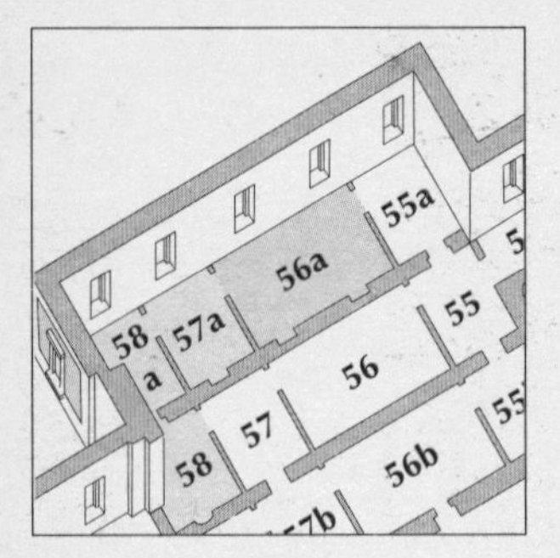

HIERONYMUS VAN AEKEN, 'BOSCH' (COPY?)
Temptation of St. Anthony

HIERONYMUS VAN AEKEN, 'BOSCH'
Temptation of St. Anthony

HIERONYMUS VAN AEKEN, 'BOSCH'
The Garden of Earthly Delights

SCHOOL OF HIERONYMUS VAN AEKEN, 'BOSCH'
Crossbowman

HIERONYMUS VAN AEKEN, 'BOSCH'
The Seven Deadly Sins

HIERONYMUS VAN AEKEN, 'BOSCH'
Curing Folly

HIERONYMUS VAN AEKEN, 'BOSCH'
Triptych: **Adoration of the Magi**

HIERONYMUS VAN AEKEN, 'BOSCH'
Triptych: **The Hay-Wain**

HIERONYMUS VAN AEKEN, 'BOSCH' (copy?)
Temptation of St. Anthony
(Cat. No. 2913)

This painting is not usually catalogued as by the artist, nor even mentioned. Some think it a copy of a lost original. There is another one like it at the Rijksmuseum in Amsterdam, but of much poorer quality. In the foreground, the saint cradles his head in meditation at a table while to his right there lowers a very odd hybrid grotesque with the head of what other pictures have taught us to understand as an old whoremonger. The female nude at the door is the stock image for a temptress, while the sign of the swan is that of a brothel. A number of typically-Bosch-like symbols are strewn about this painting which, his or not, is not devoid of merit. While some think it an original, most agree that it is an almost contemporary copy.

HIERONYMUS VAN AEKEN, 'BOSCH'
Temptation of St. Anthony
(Cat. No. 2049)

A late work and undeniably his own, it can be dated c. 1510. It is a most painstaking and accomplished piece that argues tremendous technical skill in both the figure of the saint itself and the overall colour scheme with its delicate blends of earthy greens and browns. The image of the monk as he mediates, wrapped in a cloak bearing the T standing for the order of St. Anthony, is striking in its serenity. Beside him there is a pig with a bell, this being one of the familiar symbols in his hagiography. Rather than *Temptations*, maybe the work would be better titled *Contemplations of St. Anthony,* for despite the presence of all manner of threatening traps and snares brandished by a mob of unnerving monstrosities such as the head and clawed hand reaching out from the water to scare or slash the holy man, his distilled tranquillity of soul is what pervades the picture.

The simple landscape with its streams and becks, little huts for the monks, green swards, trees and background city is a far cry from the arid abode of the real ascetic but this was how he was shown then and for many years more to come.

HIERONYMUS VAN AEKEN, 'BOSCH'
The Garden of Earthly Delights (Cat. No. 2823)

Here we have one of the most extraordinary, fantastical, and mysterious paintings in the history of art. Few paintings have given rise to such contradictory, imaginative, and outrageous explanations. No one who glances at it, could ever feel indifferent to it. Yet we know almost nothing about it from contemporary documental sources. What was its original name? When it reached El Escorial, it was

described as "a painting on the variety of life", and the monk Father Sigüenza would only refer to it as the painting "of the strawberries". Depending on whom we want Bosch to be, we find one explanation or another. If we agree with Philip II or José Sigüenza (the Hieronymite monk who described the monastery at El Escorial and showed such a positive attitude towards the artist), the general idea is fairly clear. When closed, a vision of the universe created by God, shown small upper left is seen. Some verses from the Book of Psalms make all clear: *Ipse dixit et facta sunt. Ipse mandavit et creata sunt* ("He himself said it, and so it was done. He himself ordered it, and so it was created"). Here we have the third day on which an Earthly Paradise was made. Once the work of Creation is over, we see the earthly paradise along with its crowning glory: Adam and Eve. The foreshadowing of the appearance of sin is seen in the aggressive monsters who break in upon the harmony established by the Creator. Just as in Jean de Mandeville, the fraudulent XIV Century traveller and author of a book so successful that it must have been heard of even in s'Hertogenbosch, the devil can o be seen astride the anthropomorphic rock in which the Tree of Sin is rooted. The image is so striking that Dali used it to inspire the strange form that appears in various of his works and most especially in his Great Masturbator. The middle panel describes mankind's pursuit of all manner of pleasures, especially those of the flesh and his joyful giving full rein to them. This is the focus of all attention; a world that is a flight of human, animal, vegetable, and mineral fantasy, peopled with naked groups in poses that leave nothing to our imagination. We see fantastical buildings based on familiar forms puffed up out of all proportion, and fleshy, succulent man-sized pieces of fruit. Bosch drew on many sources to forge his strangest of worlds but never merely copied, re-tempering all he took until it became all but unrecognizable. These fallen human creatures are obviously condemned to Hell and, if there are any doubts as to this, it is displayed on the right a weird place, the apotheosis of the Beauty of Wickedness and all centred upon the most ambiguous creature that even he had ever conceived. But is it truly as simple as all that? Even if it were, the world of images, symbols, and shapes created in that middle area has no equal anywhere. And needless to say, nothing whatsoever is merely gratuitous or simply ornamental. Here is where we find the richness of the painter's (and his hypothetical mentor's) figurative knowledge of literature, illustrated manuscripts, painting, marginal sculpture, etc., as well as his ability to create a private universe that has always fascinated subsequent generations of artists.

SCHOOL OF HIERONYMUS VAN AEKEN, 'BOSCH'
Crossbowman (Cat. No. 2695)

A small panel showing a human head like that of the soldiers in many others depicting Christ being crowned with thorns, a subject that fascinated the master towards the end of his life and gave us the masterpieces in the London National Gallery and the San Lorenzo de El Escorial. Monastery. Though the Prado's catalogues have always claimed it to be an original, it is generally held to be a studio copy or even one made still later like so many others to be found in both museums and collections. The Crowning with Thorns as a whole was also much imitated. And some of the copies made from it can also be seen in Spain.

HIERONYMUS VAN AEKEN, 'BOSCH'
The Seven Deadly Sins (Cat. No. 2822)

For a long time thought to be an early work, this is now supposed to date from around 1500 and so from the middle years of his career. The unequal quality of its parts could well mean it was a joint effort or studio piece. The dominant theme is expressed through God's eye (a picture of Christ against a blue background). An inscription further explains this : *Cave, cave, Dominus videt* ("Watch out, watch out, God is watching"). Around the eye a circular band splits up into seven areas, each containing a scene depicting one of the deadly sins. The sinners are under God's gaze. They are further warned by verses from Deuteronomy to bear in mind the four last expectations of Man's estate: Death, Judgement, Hell or Heaven, these being clearly pictured one to each of the four corners. This solemnly geometric layout, along with a few contemporary sources, has led many to imagine that this work of art is a tabletop. There are however as many reasons for rejecting this and seeing it as just a rectangular panel to be hung on a wall as a focus for Christian meditation which is probably what Philip II used it as at El Escorial when this was under construction, for he had it put in his private quarters there in 1574.

Hitherto, this had not been the usual way to depict the seven deadly sins. Not only does the painting's circular layout mark a break with what went before but likewise another departure is the choice of scenes of everyday life to typify the sins rather than the by then hackneyed stock personalizations of them couched in a more metaphoric language. There were other works like this one done from the early 15th century onwards however. Worthy of note are the subtlety shown in the portrayal of Envy, the invention to the pleasure-house setting for Lust, and the stark realism with which justice is to be seen meeted out in Avarice.

HIERONYMUS VAN AEKEN, 'BOSCH'
Curing Folly
(Cat. No. 2056)

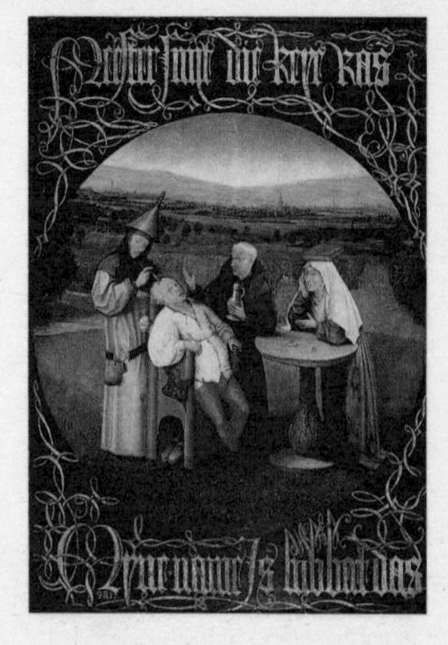

This is thought to be one of his early pieces (c. 1475-1480). It belongs to a type of intentionally satirical paintings and engravings that were common in the Low Countries at the time. A legend written in Gothic letters says "Master cuts out the stone - my name is Lubbert das" the name here apparently meaning 'little gelded man' which also has the sense of 'simpleton' in Flanders. The operation is being performed before a small audience. The quack doctor, crowned with a funnel, removes the stone from the head of a fat, old man who gazes out at us. A friar seems to sketch a blessing, while an old woman, who is balancing a book on her head, stares at the farce in bored contempt. There are no doubts as to its authenticity. It belonged to Felipe de Guevara, the great diplomat and collector, and after his death came to belong to Philip II. The scene is a fit subject for the kind of satire and criticism popular during the period from the 15th century onwards in Northern Europe.

HIERONYMUS VAN AEKEN, 'BOSCH'
Triptych: **Adoration of the Magi** (Cat. No. 2048)

This is perhaps the most beautiful and refined of all of Bosch's paintings even if others, like *The Garden of Earthly Delights*, surpass it in imagination and iconagraphical complexity. We would be hard-pressed indeed to find greater attention to form. Note the detail of jewellery in each of the objects brought by the kings. The sweeping background landscape, all done in delicate hues, is enhanced by the very high pitched viewpoint which by no means matches up with the perspective used for the figures in the story. The quality of the lush fabrics is also outstanding. Despite its title, the triptych is loaded with symbolism. For instance,

Epiphany as the manifestation of the Child's divinity, is intimated by means of a series of barely-visible vignettes. It both heralds His coming in the Old Testament and foreshadows his future Passion. Thus, the odd piece over the second king's shoulders shows Solomon's meeting with the Queen of Sheba, a common subject in which the Old Testament prefigures the New. This was common practice at the time as in the widely-spread Pauperum Bible. However, one of the crowns set on the ground shows the story of the sacrifice of Isaac, which foretells the death of Christ. This foretelling is strengthened by a reading of the triptych when closed, where a mass of St. Gregory is shown alongside a cycle of the Passion in a fanciful, almost monochromatic setting. This whole coherent world falls asunder with the strange character seen behind the kings. Apparently crowned, and half nude, he looks intently at the goings-on. Many explanations have been given to identify this figure. Perhaps he is the Antichrist whose future coming was foretold (and non-too distant future as several circles in the Low Countries believed at the time). In that sense, he offsets the Child; his headpiece is mockingly reminiscent of a crown of thorns as befits such a one who would go fly in the face of Christ. The complex Epiphany is here transformed in a genre work with the added touch of having Saint Joseph, who has disappeared from the central panel, off in the left one where he is drying the infant's clouts. This, far from indicating artistic adventursomeness, merely shows how little importance his figure was allowed in those times – a matter soon to change. The shepherd's reaction to the presence of the Three Kings goes well beyond curiosity to become quite disquieting. The coats of arms that have led to the donors being identified, line the sides beside their patrons Peter and Agnes. The whole piece bears a clear signature. The date is believed to be c. 1510, late in the artist's career.

HIERONYMUS VAN AEKEN, 'BOSCH' Triptych:
The Hay-Wain (Cat. No. 2052)

Although of poor quality, this is one of Bosch's most famous paintings. Even so, it is considered to be an authentic work, its unevenness being put down to restorations and the tolls of time. There is another copy in the Escorial of even worse painterly quality. There is general agreement that it was inspired by the verses from Isaiah (XL, 6-7): "All flesh is grass and all its goodness is like a flower in the fields. The grass dries and the flower droops". Homely Bosch or his mentor may have also added some Flemish proverb on the same idea to the brew. When closed, the triptych shows a wretched and melancholic old man hobbling along a path that leads through scenes of atrocity. He represents the eternal pilgrim down the Road of Life and may have been drawn from the immensely popular and many times illustrated work of William Deguilleville, *Pélerinage de la vie humaine*. Once opened, the triptych reveals the classical three-panel set. It begins with the Creation, sin and the fall from grace, and our fore-fathers banishment from Paradise. The centre piece shows the hay-wain being followed by one and all while the last panel offers a glimpse of Hell where sinners are getting their just deserts. The hay-wain is the focal point of the triptych. It is huge and overloaded.It is being drawn by monstrous creatures, and followed by the peoples of

the Earth, led by a pope and an emperor. On top, we see a kind of 'garden of love' flanked by an angel and a devil. The angel gazes up at a cloudburst of glory where Christ leans out in judgement. The devil is meanwhile engrossed in the musical and sexual follies going on. The lower zones are crowded with scenes depicting a variety of deadly sins (the wain top shows Lust). Some of the sins are, even by today's standards, given very graphic expression. The hay, used to express both variety and transience, in nevertheless attractively portrayed.

Other Flemish Paintings other than the Prado's.

Since there are so many artists, it is hard to mention even the most significant paintings other than the Prado's so we will limit ourselves to those that have a major universal relevance and some of the more important ones hanging in other Spanish collections, museums, and churches.

Jan van Eyck's work is fairly scarce. His most famous work is the *Polyptych of the Adoration of the Lamb* in St. Bavo's in Ghent. His religious paintings include *The Virgin with Chancellor Rolin* (Louvre), *The Virgin with Canon van der Paele* (Bruges), and the *Triptych of Dresden*. portraits such as: *Giovanni Arnolfini and his Wife* (National Gal., London), *Cardinal Albergatti* (Vienna), *Man with Turban* (National Gal., London). Religious works: *Annunciation* (Thyssen Mus., Madrid), *St. Barbara* (Royal Mus., Brussels). Sources speak of paintings that were famous in their day, but have now disappeared, such as a St. George belonging to Alfonso V, and a map of the World that provoked general amazement.

Of Robert Campin, allegedly the Master of Flemalle's work, the list is even shorter, especially now as doubt has been cast on his authorship of the *Mérode Triptych* (Cloisters Mus., New York). Earlier pieces: the *Seilem Triptych* (Courtauld Institute, London), *The Virgin, St. Veronica,* and *The Holy Trinity* (Städel Institute, Frankfort). Later pieces: *Nativity* (Dijon), portraits of a *man* and *woman* (National Gal., London), and of a *man* (Thyssen Mus., Madrid). The only documented work directly attributable to him is what remains of the colouring to sculptor Jean Delemer's *Annunciation* in Tournai Cathedral.

Roger van der Weyden's list of works is still under discussion. Questions have been raised as to the authorship of two very similar triptychs : *Miraflores* (Berlin) and *Granada* (Royal Chapel of Granada, and Metropolitan Mus., New York), experts at

present only accept *Miraflores.* Religious pieces: *Crucifixion* (Monastery of El Escorial), the *Columba Triptych* with the Epiphany (Munich), *Triptych of the Seven Sacraments* (Brussels), *Lamentation* (Galleria Ufizzi, Florence), *Diptych of the Crucifixion* (Johnson Col., Philadelphia), *Virgin* (Thyssen Mus., Madrid), *Altarpiece of Pierre Bladellin* (Berlin). Portraits: *Antoine, Grand Bâtard de Bourgogne* (Royal Mus., Brussels), *Young Woman* (National Gal., Washington). Largest work: *Polyptych of the Last Judgement* (Beaune Hospital). Most famous lost work: *Justice of Trajan and of Herkenbald* (City Hall, Brussels).
The catalogue of the works of Petrus Christus has remained much the same for years. Portraits: *Carthusian* (Metropolitan Mus., New York), *Young Man* (National Gal., London). Religious pieces: *St. Eloy* (Metropolitan Mus., New York), *Madonna of the Dry Tree* (Thyssen Mus., Madrid), *Lamentation* (Royal Mus., Brussels).
Dieric Bouts's two most famous pieces are the Triptych of the Last Supper at Louvain Cathedral and the two large paintings on the 'Justice of the Emperor Otto III' (Royal Mus., Brussels), one of these finished by his disciples. Unjustly ignored is the splendid *Triptych of the Descent* (Royal Chapel, Granada). Other noteworthy pieces: *Virgin and Child enthroned between Angels* (Royal Chapel, Granada), *The Blessed and the Damned* (wings of a triptych whose central *Last Judgement* has been lost, at the Lille Mus.), *Entombment* (National Gal., London), *Triptych of the Epiphany,* the 'Pearl of Brabant' (Munich).
Weyden's follower Vrancke van der Stockt has a *Last Judgement* (Town Hall, Valencia), an excellent *Presentation in the Temple* (Monastery of El Escorial), and *Lamentation* (van der Burgh, Antwerp). By the Master of the Legend of St. Catherine, the paintings depicting the story his name is taken from (private col., Geneva) and the *Altarpiece of Job* (Wallraf-Richartz, Cologne).

Hans Memling must have been quite prolific; the list of his many paintings is now being tidied up with perhaps with overly stringent criteria. His most popular piece (though not his best) is the *Shrine of St. Ursula* (St. John's Hospital, Bruges). His large triptychs: *Last Judgement* (Pomorskie Mus., Gdansk), *The Mystic Marriage of St. Catherine* (St. John's Hospital, Bruges), and *Donne* (National Gal., London). Other diptychs or single paintings: the *Diptych of the Descent* (Royal Chapel, Granada), *The Flagellation of Christ at the Column* (Mateu Col., Barcelona), *The Seven Joys of Mary* (Pinothek, Munich), *Passion of Christ* (Sabauda Gall., Turin). Portraits: *Maarten van Nieuwenhove Diptych* (St. John's Hospital, Bruges), *Young Man* (Thyssen Mus., Madrid), *Man with a Coin* (Antwerp Mus.).
Gerard David's work is extensive and may even include illuminated books. Most noteworthy: *Crucifixion* (Berlin), *Adoration of the Magi* (Pinakothek, Munich), *Altarpiece of the Baptism of Christ* (Groninge Mus., Bruges), *Mystic Marriage of St. Catherine* (National Gal., London). Special mention should be made of his 'Justice Panels' (Groninge Mus., Bruges) along the lines of work by Weyden and Bouts.
In contrast, Bosch's list of works is quite short, and several of his best are in the Prado. Others outside the museum but in Spain are *Crowning with Thorns* (El Escorial), *St. John the Baptist* (Lázaro Galdiano Mus., Madrid), and *Christ Carrying the Cross* (Royal Palace, Madrid). On a par with the best, the *Temptation of St. Anthony* (Lisbon). Another important collection is in the Doge's Palace in Venice, with the *Triptych of the Hermits* and the four paintings of the *Damned and the Blessed.* Among other pieces: *Crowning with Thorns* (National Gal., London), *Christ Carrying the Cross* (Ghent), the misnamed *Prodigal Son* (Boymans Mus., Rotterdam).

Basic time line

1404: Death of Philip the Bold, Duke of Burgundy, succeeded by John the Fearless.

1419: John the Fearless assassinated, Philip the Good named Duke of Burgundy.

1425: Jan van Eyck enters the service of Philip the Good.

1427: Rogelet de la Pasture (Roger van der Weyden) begins his apprenticeship under Robert Campin.

1428: A Burgundian embassy including van Eyck leaves for Portugal to arrange marriage between Philip and Isabel of Portugal.

1432: Jan van Eyck finishes Ghent's *Polyptych of the Adoration of the Lamb* started by his brother Hubert.

1435: Van der Weyden begins work in Brussels, where he is named official city painter the next year.

1441: Jan van Eyck dies in Bruges.

1444: Robert Campin, so-called Master of Flemalle, dies in Tournai.

1444: Petrus Christus becomes a citizen of Bruges.

1450: Birth of Hieronymus van Aeken, 'Bosch'.

1464: Van der Weyden dies.

1464: Dieric or Thierry Bouts contracted to do a triptych of the Last Supper for St. Peter's in Louvain.

1465: Hans Memling, German born, registers as a citizen of Bruges.

1467: Philip the Good dies, succeeded by Charles the Rash.

1468: Bouts, official painter of Louvain.

1469: Erasmus of Rotterdam born.

1473: Memling sends a large triptych of the Last Judgement to Angelo Tani, but the ship carrying it is taken by Corsairs out of Gdansk or Dantzig.

1475: Bouts dies, leaving the second panel of the Justice of Emperor Otto III unfinished.

1477: Charles the Rash dies in the Battle of Nancy, the Duchy of Burgundy breaks up. His daughter, Mary of Burgundy, wife of Maximilian, inherits the Low Countries.

1478: Hugo van der Goes retires to Rouge-Cloître in Auderhem.

1489: Memling finishes the reliquary of St. Ursula for St. John's Hospital in Bruges.

1494: Sebastian Brant publishes *his Das Narrenschiff* illustrated by many engravings.

1495: Marriage of Margaret of Austria and Philip the Handsome, children of the emperor Maximilian, to John of Aragón and Joan the Mad, children of Ferdinand and Isabella.

Bibliography

General

Friedländer, M.: *Early Netherlandish painting,* Leyden and Brussels, 1967-1976, 14 vols.

Panofsky, E.: *Early Netherlandish painting,* Cambridge (Mass.), 1953, 2 vols.

Philippot, P.: *La peinture dans les anciens Pays- Bas, XV-XVIe. siécles,* París, 1994.

Pächt, O.: *Altniederländische Malerei,* München, 1994.

A.A.V.V.: *Les primitifs flamands et leur temps,* New Louvain, 1994.

Châtelet, A.: *Les primitifs hollandais,* Freiburg, 1980.

Lane, B.G.: *The altar and the alterpiece. Sacramental themes in early netherlandish painting,* New York, 1984.

Campbell, L.: "The art market in the Southern Netherlands in the fifteenth century", in *Burlington Magazine,* CXVIII (1968), pp. 186 ss.

Monographs

Dhanens, E.: *Hubert et Jan van Eyck,* Antwerp, 1980.

Yarza Luaces, J.: *Jan van Eyck,* Madrid, 1993.

Pächt, O.: *Van Eyck and the Founders of Early Netherlandish Painting,* London, 1994.

Châtelet, A.: *L'atelier de Robert Campin,* en *Les Grandes siécles de Tournai,* Tournai-Louvain, 1993, pp. 13-40.

Châtelet, André: *Robert Campin, le Maître de Flémalle,* Antwerp, 1996.

Davies, M.: *Rogier van der Weyden,* London, 1972.

Rogier van der Weyden-Roger de la Pasture, peintre officiel de la ville de Bruxelles, Exhibition, Brussels, 1979.

Dieric Bouts, Brussels, 1957.

Smeyers, Maurits: *Dirk Bouts,* Tournai, 1998.

De Vos, D.: *Hans Memling. L'oeuvre complete*, Antwerp, 1994.

De Vos *et al.*: *Hans Memling, Catalogue*, Bruges and Antwerp, 1994.

De Vos (ed.): *Hans Memling, Essays*, Bruges, 1994.

Upton, J.: *Petrus Christus. His place in fifteenth century flemish painting*, University Park and London, 1990.

Van Miegroet, H.J.: *Gerard David*, Antwerp-Paris, 1990.

Tolnay, Ch. de: *Jérome Bosch. L'oeuvre complète*, Paris, 1989 (1937).

Gibson, W.S.: *El Bosco*, Barcelona, 1993.

Bango, I., Marías, F.: *Bosch. Realidad, símbolo y fantasía*, Madrid, 1982.

Marijnissen, R. *et. al.*: *Iheronimus Bosch*, Brussels, 1972.

Yarza Luaces, J.: *Los pecados capitales del Bosco*, en *Obras maestras del Museo del Prado*, Madrid, 1996, pp. 87-103.

Yarza Luaces, J.: *El Jardín de las Delicias de El Bosco*, Madrid, 1998.

General Information on the Prado Museum

EDIFICIO VILLANUEVA
Paseo del Prado, s/n
28014 Madrid
Telephone:
91 330.28.00
Fax:
91 330.28.56
Information:
91 330.29.00
Wheelchair access available

VISITING HOURS
Tuesday through Saturday:
9:00 a.m. to 7:00 p.m.
Sundays and holidays:
9:00 a.m. to 2:00 p.m.
Closed on *Mondays*

ENTRANCE FEES
General Admission *3 euros*

Spanish youth card, student card, or international equivalents.
Cultural and education group rates (by advance request)
91 330.28.25 *1,5 euros*

Senior citizens over 65 or pensioners.
Members of the Fundación Amigos del Museo del Prado.
Cultural and educational volunteers
Free

Free General Admission Days
Saturdays, from 2:30 p.m. to 7:00 p.m.
Sundays, from 9:00 a.m. to 2:00 p.m.

Coffee Shop
Tuesday to Saturday:
9:30 a.m. to 6:30 p.m.
Sundays and holidays:
9:30 a.m. to 1:30 p.m.

Restaurant
Monday to Saturday:
9:30 a.m. to 6:30 p.m.

Shops
Tuesday to Saturday:
9:30 a.m. to 6:30 p.m.
Sundays and holidays:
9:30 a.m. to 1:30 p.m.

HOW TO GET THERE
Metro:
Atocha, Banco and Retiro stations

Bus:
Numbers 9, 10, 14, 19, 27, 34, 37, 45

From the airport:
Airport shuttle bus to Plaza de Colón, then No. 27 bus

General Information about the Fundación Amigos del Museo del Prado
Museo del Prado
c/ Ruiz de Alarcón, nº 21 – bajo. 28014 Madrid
Tel.: 91 420.20.46
Fax.: 91 429.50.20
E-mail: famprado@canaldata.es

Office hours:
Monday to Friday, from 9:30 a.m. to 2:30 p.m.